Intersections:
Where Faith and Life Meet

A Cumberland Presbyterian Adult Resource
Volume 4, Lent, Easter, & Pentecost

Discipleship Ministry Team
Ministry Council
Cumberland Presbyterian Church

8207 Traditional Place
Cordova, Tennessee 38016

First Edition 2015

Published by The Discipleship Ministry Team
General Assembly Ministry Council of the Cumberland Presbyterian Church
Cordova, Tennessee

ISBN-13: 978-0692381687

ISBN-10: 0692381686

We want to hear from you.
Please send your comments about this curriculum to
the Discipleship Ministry Team at chm@cumberland.org.

OUR UNITED OUTREACH
Made Possible In Part By Your Tithe To Our United Outreach

Table of Contents

Editor: Cindy Martin
Designer: Joanna Wilkinson
Proofreader: Mark Taylor

To order, call 901-276-4572, x 252 or e-mail resources@cumberland.org.

Who Am I?

Scripture for lesson:
Luke 3:15-17, 21-22

Define identity. What factors help you determine your identity? How do you help others form their identities?

Prep for the Journey

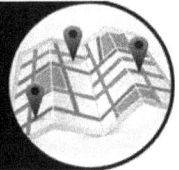

Identity. It's a catch phrase in our society, something we seek to learn about ourselves and others. The people in our nation tend to judge people based on first impressions. Our society limits one's identity to profession, age, or marital status. So I ask, is this the way we, as a people of faith, define identity?

On the Road

In our scripture for this lesson, John's preaching had gathered a group of faithful people. These men and women were children of Israel, and they had heard John's teachings on judgment and justice. They saw him as a great leader—perhaps a little out of the ordinary with his camel-skin clothing and diet of locust and wild honey, but great nonetheless. As they listened to his words, the questions began to stir within them: "Could this man be the one for whom we have been waiting? Is he the Messiah?"

Read Luke 3:15-17.

As the people were filled with expectation, and all were questioning in their hearts concerning John, whether he might be the Messiah, [16] *John answered all of them by saying, "I baptize you with water; but one who is more powerful than I is coming; I am not worthy to untie the thong of his sandals. He will baptize you with the Holy Spirit and fire.* [17] *His winnowing fork is in his hand, to clear his threshing floor and to gather the wheat into his granary; but the chaff he will burn with unquenchable fire."*

John was quick to answer that he was not the Messiah but a prophet who had come to prepare the way for the Messiah. However, since the people were so interested, he eagerly gave them some clues as to the identity of the Messiah. "The one who is coming," John said, "is far greater than I. He will baptize you with the Holy Spirit."

John was sure of his identity and the call that God had placed upon his life. Out of this knowledge of his identity, John was able to proclaim to the people, "Repent. Get right with God. God is sending your salvation, so get ready. God's going to give you the Holy Spirit, the same spirit that was with the prophets of old. The Messiah is coming, and he's going to call you to task. Will you be the productive wheat, or will you be blown into the fire?"

John's comments point to a religious experience that is beyond our control. Because it arises from a responsiveness to what God is doing among us, such an experience cannot be channeled or domesticated to our tastes. God calls for a genuine repentance and a commitment to the lifestyle of a covenant people.

Scenic Route

John's bold preaching led to his arrest by Herod (verse 20), effectively ending John's ministry as told in Luke's Gospel. It also sets the stage for another man to begin his ministry. And how does that ministry start? Why, with a claiming of identity!

Read Luke 3:21-22.

Now when all the people were baptized, and when Jesus also had been baptized and was praying, the heaven was opened, ²² and the Holy Spirit descended upon him in bodily form like a dove. And a voice came from heaven, "You are my Son, the Beloved; with you I am well pleased."

Jesus was with a group of people who were being baptized. Jesus was baptized as well. Nothing out of the ordinary, so far. Then Jesus began to pray. We do not know the words of Jesus' prayer. We cannot tell what kind of prayer it was, but the response to this prayer was nothing short of amazing. The heavens opened. If closing the heavens brought a drought such as the one that lasted for three years in Elijah's time, then opening the heavens would have brought God's blessings. It would have signified that God's power and mercy was about to be unleashed, so hold on!

And what comes down from the heavens? The Holy Spirit, which was poured out like a dove upon Jesus. Jesus, being both fully human and fully divine, already had an intimate and complete relationship with the Holy Spirit as a member of the Trinity. It is my belief that the

What does it mean to be committed to the lifestyle of a covenant people? What is a covenant? How do you show genuine repentance?

So what about our identities? How are we more than our occupation or vocation? In a world that is quick to define and choose and judge, how do we help one another define our identities and those of our children?

What does the phrase "family of God" mean to you? How do we, as the family of God, help one another develop an identity in Christ?

How can those who are young in their faith learn how to tithe if you do not show the way? How can the children learn the love and call to missions if you will not get your hands and feet dirty? How can they learn the joy of service and forgiveness if you will not help one another or open your hearts to forgive?

action of the Holy Spirit at this particular time was like an anointing, a consecration, and an ordination for service. It was a confirmation of the calling to which Jesus was responding. And as if the heavens opening and the Holy Spirit descending were not enough to convince us of his identity, a voice called out from heaven.

We are not told if others could hear the voice, or if it was a voice Jesus alone heard. Either way, the words were pivotal to Jesus' work in the world, and to our faith. "You are my Son, the Beloved," the voice called. "With you I am well pleased." The identity of Jesus as God's son had been announced earlier in Luke. (See Luke 2:11, 25-32, 49.) A voice from heaven affirmed those earlier announcements. With his identity confirmed, Jesus could begin his ministry. He could go about the work of the kingdom, empowered by the Holy Spirit and those precious words of a parent. Jesus' identity was prophecy fulfilled; it was confirmed by God and the Holy Spirit.

Workers Ahead — CAUTION

The words of the voice from heaven serve as a reminder that declarations of a parent's love and affirmation of the child are vital to any child's development. Any child who strives to affirm his or her own identity and self-worth without having heard that affirmation from his or her parents faces intense struggles. We who are made in the image of God, and whom God calls as co-creators in the process of birth, are obligated in return to emulate God by blessing those with whom God entrusts us. We are to build up one another. We are to give words of love and encouragement to one another. Our responsibility to bless is not limited to our biological children, but includes those children who have been given to us as the community of faith.

Those who comprise the church are a family. Most of us have heard the church referred to as a family on multiple occasions.

Look at the person sitting next to you. Don't just glance because you already know the person, but take time truly to look at him or her. That person is your sister, your brother. These are your peers, your accountability, your partners in God's work.

Those of you who are young, look around. These people are your mother and father, your grandmother and grandfather. Love them, respect them, pray for them, and trust them. God gave them to you as role models in this family of faith. Take care of them as they age and grieve. You are their hope for the future and their joy in today.

Those of you who are older, look around. These people are your sons and daughters, your grandchildren and great-grandchildren. Love them, respect them, pray for them, and trust them. God gave them to you, and they are your responsibility. You are to guide them, and teach them what it means to claim an identity in Christ. You do not get to retire from this work. We are family; you don't retire from family.

We should strive to be children of our faith communities—to want to sit at one another's feet, hear one another's stories, learn from one another's mistakes, and experience the joy of family. We should strive to be parents to this congregation—to want to care for others when they are hurt; to teach others what God needs them to learn; to let others know when we are proud of them; and to correct them as needed. We should strive to be siblings to our community of faith—to want to walk beside one another in the faith—learning, exploring, and feasting on God's goodness every day. These things form our Christian identity.

In the Rear View

Identity is so important. It is our common identity that calls us together as the body of Christ. It is our common identity that calls us to the Lord's Table. It is our common identity that calls us as children invited to the feast. Pray together that throughout this journey of Lent you may begin to experience identity as God's child in new and exciting ways. May you strive to hear the words, "This is my child, in whom I am well pleased."

How can you as individuals and as a community of faith actively walk with one another, showing one another your shared identity as children of God? List ways in which this is already happening and areas in which you could begin to do so.

Travel Log

Day 1:

List ten words that define you. Are these the same words others would use to describe you? Ask a friend for three to five words that describe you. List them as well. How does your friend's list agree with, or differ from, your thoughts?

1)	1)
2)	2)
3)	3)
4)	4)
5)	5)
6)	
7)	
8)	
9)	
10)	

Day 2:

John knew his identity. He was literally set aside from birth to fulfill the role of prophet. How easy do you think it was for him? What caused him to continue on this path? God has a calling in each of our lives. Spend time today asking God what your calling is. Write down any impressions or thoughts God gives you.

Day 3:

What does "Beloved child of God" mean to you? How are you living into that role? In what ways are you treating others as beloved children of God? On what areas do you need to work? Who do you need to remind of their identity in Christ today? Journal your responses to the questions.

Day 4:

Make a list of people who have helped to form your Christian identity. Pray for each of these individuals. Then list those individuals whose Christian identity you have an opportunity to help shape. Pray for each of them today.

Day 5:

Sometimes it is easy to fall into the role of savior for others. The crowds asked John if he was the Messiah; they would easily have accepted him as such. Instead, John pointed the searchers toward the true Messiah.

How does your life point others toward Jesus? If others only saw your actions from Monday to Saturday, would they know you had a relationship with Christ? Think of at least two ways that you can live a life that points more directly towards Jesus as Lord. Record your ideas below. Look back in a couple of weeks to see how successful you have been in implementing these ideas.

Day 6:

Read Luke 2:21-22. What words stand out to you? Is there anything in these verses you have not noticed before? Jesus was praying when he heard the words from God.

How important is your prayer life in helping form and sustain your identity as a child of God? We cannot know the will of God if we do not spend time with God. Take time throughout the day to talk with God. Perhaps you could pray on your way to work or at every stop light you encounter. Intentionally spend time listening to God's words for you. Write down some of your impressions from this exercise.

Day 7:

How do you respond to God's call in your life? Are you ready and willing, or are you slow to act? Jot down some times when you have felt God asking you to do something, and record how you responded. Reflect about those times. As you look at what you have noted, is there a pattern that might show you where God is leading?

Fighting with Temptation

Scripture for lesson:
Luke 4:1-13

Prep for the Journey

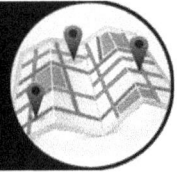

The temptation of Jesus is familiar to many of us, so why talk about it again? Why bring up the temptation year after year during Lent?

It's simple; temptation never goes away. Just look at Luke 4:13, "He [the devil] departed from him until an opportune time." As Christians, we do not just have to overcome temptation once or twice. Temptation comes back time and time again, never letting us get truly comfortable.

On the Road

Let me try to "paint a picture" of what giving in to temptation does to our relationship with God. Each time we give in to temptation, we build a wall between ourselves and God. Each time we lie, we add another brick. Each time we choose our comfort over loving others, we add another brick. Each time we seek to serve ourselves rather than serving others, we add another brick. Eventually we separate ourselves from God. We reach the point where we do not see or hear God; neither do we seek God. God is still there, but we have drawn away from our Creator. And, my friends, building walls is an easy thing to do—easier than we like to admit.

Read Luke 4:1-4.
Jesus, full of the Holy Spirit, returned from the Jordan and was led by the Spirit in the wilderness, ² where for forty days he was tempted by the devil. He ate nothing at all during those days, and when they were

---

What temptations recur in your life? How do you handle their recurrence?

over, he was famished. [3] *The devil said to him, "If you are the Son of God, command this stone to become a loaf of bread."* [4] *Jesus answered him, "It is written, 'One does not live by bread alone.'"*

Through his responses, Jesus has shown us how to handle all types of temptation. He had been fasting for forty days, completely without food. He was bound to have been weak from hunger when the devil approached him with the simplest of suggestions: "I'm sure you're hungry. Why don't you turn these stones into bread?"

There is nothing inherently evil about having food. After all, your body needs nourishment to survive. *It would not have hurt Jesus to have had just a tiny bite of bread*, some may think. God doesn't begrudge anyone food! What's the harm in a few carbs? But Jesus replied, "One does not live by bread alone." Nourishment comes in many forms, and Jesus had been driven into the desert by the Holy Spirit to feast on God, not bread. The manna he ate was fellowship with God.

I wonder if Jesus' response frustrated the devil. He had tempted the woman and man in the Garden of Eden with fruit. Even though they had access to all kinds of food, they desired the one thing that was off limits. So the devil started with food, appealing to a basic human need, but was quickly shut down. So he tried harder.

Read Luke 4:5-8.

Then the devil led him up and showed him in an instant all the kingdoms of the world. [6] *And the devil said to him, "To you I will give their glory and all this authority; for it has been given over to me, and I give it to anyone I please.* [7] *If you, then, will worship me, it will all be yours."* [8] *Jesus answered him, "It is written,*

'Worship the Lord your God,
and serve only him.'"

The devil showed Jesus all the kingdoms of the world and told him that they could all be his—every corner of the earth. All Jesus had to do was worship the devil. We read this temptation and think, of course Jesus said no. This was a no-brainer. But let's look at this a little more closely.

What the devil offered Jesus was Jesus' main goal: a world saved entirely, redeemed completely, wholly his. And all he had to do was pay tribute to the devil. He wouldn't have to be scorned by his family and friends, he wouldn't have to be beaten or executed on the cross. All he would have had to do was say a few words of worship and poof, goal accomplished.

But Jesus knew this was a ploy. He knew that worshiping anything or anyone other than God is like trying to ride a bike with square wheels—pointless. "Worship the Lord your God and serve only him." These words are more than just a good quote from the Torah or the Ten Commandments; they are words by which Jesus lived, ones by which we should live as well. Jesus knew his life would be lived in service, and that through his service he would point others to the Way, the truth, and the light!

Why do you think the devil first chose to tempt Jesus with bread? How often do you feel tempted by the most basic of human needs?

When are you tempted to take the easy way out? How often do you try shortcuts to healing or spiritual wellness? How difficult do you think this temptation was to resist?

Read Luke 4:9-12.

Then the devil took him to Jerusalem, and placed him on the pinnacle of the temple, saying to him, "If you are the Son of God, throw yourself down from here, [10] for it is written,

> *'He will command his angels concerning you,*
> > *to protect you,'*

[11] and

> *'On their hands they will bear you up,*
> > *so that you will not dash your foot against a stone.'"*

[12] Jesus answered him, "It is said, 'Do not put the Lord your God to the test.'"

The devil changed tactics and rushed Jesus off to the Temple where he offered Jesus the chance to reveal himself to the whole of Jerusalem. If he would just throw himself off the top of the Temple, the angels would rescue him if he were indeed the Son of God. I think this offer might have been the most tempting to Jesus. It didn't involve breaking a commandment, or even a commitment. It didn't entail denying who he was or what he was there to do. In fact it seems to be another easy out, a way to show who he was without all of the pain and hurt that would come. And to top it off, the devil, who is a good biblical scholar, quoted scripture to him. I can almost hear the words of my grandma in the text, whispering in Jesus' ear, "If it looks too good to be true, it probably is!"

"Do not put the Lord your God to the test." Period. Jesus slammed the door on this line of discussion, and the devil realized that it was time to walk away.

Scenic Route

Jesus did not rely on his human strength or human understanding when dealing with temptation. The conversations recorded in this passage in Luke were more than just a theological debate between good and evil. Jesus relied upon the traditions found in scriptures to side step temptation.

These verses are a very dramatic portion of scripture. I remember seeing drawings of the temptations of Jesus in Sunday school and thinking how cool Jesus was to be able to step away from the devil and come out smelling like a rose. But then I also found myself thinking, I hope Jesus doesn't expect me to do that. I mean, after all, he *was* Jesus.

Facing temptation head-on is hard. It's even harder to get temptation to back down. If temptation was always dressed in a devil costume, we might be more able to confront it. But that's just not the case; temptation comes in endlessly different shapes and sizes.

When have you leaped when things looked good only later to discover that they were "too good to be true"? What might have kept you out of that situation? How can you keep from falling prey to such temptation again?

14

It's the simple thought that "no one will know" as you sneak another cookie or piece of candy. It's the lustful feeling you get when seeing someone drive that new car off the lot. It's the laugh that forms in your throat when you hear an off-color joke. It's the extra thirty minutes of sleep you tell yourself you need when you've set aside that time for Bible study. Temptation is anything that can lead to a separation from God—anything.

Workers Ahead

The ancient church used the forty days before Easter as a final teaching time for those who were seeking baptism. It was a way to reinforce all the lessons they had been learning during their three-year candidacy process.

Lent is the time in the Christian calendar when we look at our lives—at our temptations, at our brokenness—and we cry out to God. We ask God to help us, to restore us, and to heal us. But for healing to occur, we must examine and remove the infection. That's one of the reasons we often add a prayer of confession to Lenten worship services, if we don't always have one in the service. If we don't acknowledge our hunger, how will we be fed? If we don't acknowledge that we are sinners in need of God's grace, how will we ever accept that grace?

Lent is a time of examination, realization, and preparation. When we earnestly seek God, when we ask God to remove all boundaries, then God will break down our self-built walls. God will enter into our lives with passion, mercy, and grace, healing us and restoring us to right relationship. The journey of Lent leads us into Easter, showing us that the Resurrection was more than a miracle; it was and is God's love letter to us.

In the Rear View

Use the remaining days of Lent to examine your life. Look in the cobweb-filled corners of your heart. Seek a closer relationship with God, who has never stopped knocking on your heart's door. Remember God's sacrifice that enables us to be healed. And prepare to celebrate, really celebrate, the resurrection of Christ!

Take a few moments to list some things that get between you and God. Keep in mind that they may not be inherently "bad" things. However, the place they may have taken in your life pushes God out of the rightful place.

As a small group, or individually, spend time in prayer asking God to lead you throughout this Lenten journey. Ask God to help you claim your identity as a child of God and to help that identity inform your faith and deeds.

Day 1:

Recall those things you identified as temptations that recur in your life. What makes these things so difficult to release? What lessons have you learned from this passage in Luke that might be of help to you? Develop a plan of action to help you the next time you are faced with any of these recurring temptations. Make some notes about your plan of action.

Day 2:

Short cuts are a big part of our world. From driving to work to losing weight, we are always looking for the fastest, most efficient way of doing things. When have you been tempted to take a "spiritual short cut"? Why might doing so be a bad idea? Having a good relationship with God is about more than one or two hours a week. Note below some ways you might improve your time spent with God this week.

Day 3:

Sometimes things that keep us from God are not obvious temptations. But by placing them above God or God's instructions, they become barriers to our relationship with God. Spend time in prayer today asking God to reveal those things that you have placed before your relationship with God. Record any observations you make during this prayer time.

Day 4:

The devil left Jesus "until an opportune time." What does "opportune time" mean? Do we only have to turn away from temptation once? twice? three times? What might an "opportune time" look like for you? How can you avoid moments that might lead to such temptation? Make note of your ideas below.

Day 5:

How do you rely upon the word of God when making choices? Honestly evaluate your use of God's word. Perhaps you need to begin to memorize some scriptures or read the Bible more frequently. Write down at least two ways that will help you begin to listen more to the witness of scripture in your daily life.

Day 6:

Our Lenten journey is one that allows us to reconnect with our identities as children of God and show us what that identity means as the church. Reflect for a moment about your relationship with God during this Lenten season. How do you see your relationship growing or changing? Note areas on which you need to continue to work.

Day 7:

This wilderness experience helped Jesus prepare for his time of ministry. What moments of darkness and temptation have prepared you to serve and share God's love with others? What wonderful things has God done in your life through times of trial? Take time to thank God for these times, if you have not yet done so.

Turn of the Tide

FAITH LIFE

Scripture for lesson:
Luke 4:14-32

What have you remembered one way, only to find that it was much different than what you remembered or expected? How did you react? How did this experience affect some of your other memories or ideals?

Prep for the Journey

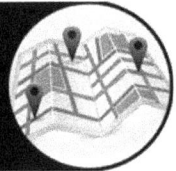

My family and I recently took a trip to Sherman, Texas, for my grandmother's funeral. While we were there, I took my kids to see the house in which my grandparents had lived, and where they had raised my father and aunt. The whole way to the house, I told them stories of how big and beautiful the house was; how the back yard had the biggest tree I'd ever seen; and that the yard went on forever. When we pulled up, my middle child looked at me and asked, "Is that it, Mommy?" The address was right, but the house looked so much smaller to my adult eyes, the yard very manageable, and the tree was less than stellar.

On the Road

Jesus made a trip home—to Nazareth. Apparently he had been busy since his temptation in the wilderness, for news of his actions had arrived ahead of him.

Read Luke 4:14-15.
Then Jesus, filled with the power of the Spirit, returned to Galilee, and a report about him spread through all the surrounding country. [15] *He began to teach in their synagogues and was praised by everyone.*

As this passage of Luke opens, we hear tales of the great things Jesus had been doing. Successful in his ministry, Jesus had returned to his hometown for a visit. You can almost hear the people buzzing with excitement over having a local celebrity in their midst. People were craning their necks, waiting to see what Jesus would do there. It would have been easy to get caught up in the hype.

Jesus' first public appearance in Nazareth was in the synagogue, where he joined the service of worship and teaching. This was a natural place for the hometown boy to go. And people couldn't wait to hear him speak.

Read Luke 4:16-22.

When he came to Nazareth, where he had been brought up, he went to the synagogue on the Sabbath day, as was his custom. He stood up to read, [17] and the scroll of the prophet Isaiah was given to him. He unrolled the scroll and found the place where it was written:
[18] *"The Spirit of the Lord is upon me,*
because he has anointed me
to bring good news to the poor.
He has sent me to proclaim release to the captives
and recovery of sight to the blind,
to let the oppressed go free,
[19] *to proclaim the year of the Lord's favor."*
[20] *And he rolled up the scroll, gave it back to the attendant, and sat down. The eyes of all in the synagogue were fixed on him. [21] Then he began to say to them, "Today this scripture has been fulfilled in your hearing." [22] All spoke well of him and were amazed at the gracious words that came from his mouth. They said, "Is not this Joseph's son?"*

What an amazing thing to have happen. Jesus was fulfilling everyone's wishes and desires. He read from the scroll of the prophet Isaiah these beautiful words of liberation and favor from the Lord. This was great news! People were nodding their heads in agreement. The thought of being liberated from Roman oppression was just what they needed to support Jesus. Freedom for the Jewish people, and freedom for the nation of Israel were patriotic and popular ideas. Jesus seemed to be claiming his role as a prophet of Israel, one who would bring about all of the things for which they had hoped! What more could one want from a hometown hero?

So, people began to build him up. They said good things about him to one another. They marveled at the fact that they knew him when he was nothing more than a carpenter's son. They were wondering just what great things he would do for them, for their town, for their nation. Surely God's favor was upon them.

When have you gotten carried away by excitement? What happened?

How do you react to hearing good news? Do you get excited, or wait for the other shoe to drop?

The people of Nazareth had enjoyed hearing Jesus' words and were awaiting his actions. After all, what good are words without deeds? Jesus had a reputation to uphold. What better place to build his reputation and the reputation of the community than in Nazareth?

Read Luke 4:23-30.

He said to them, "Doubtless you will quote to me this proverb, 'Doctor, cure yourself!' And you will say, 'Do here also in your hometown the things that we have heard you did at Capernaum.'" 24 And he said, "Truly I tell you, no prophet is accepted in the prophet's hometown. 25 But the truth is, there were many widows in Israel in the time of Elijah, when the heaven was shut up three years and six months, and there was a severe famine over all the land; 26 yet Elijah was sent to none of them except to a widow at Zarephath in Sidon. 27 There were also many lepers in Israel in the time of the prophet Elisha, and none of them was cleansed except Naaman the Syrian." 28 When they heard this, all in the synagogue were filled with rage. 29 They got up, drove him out of the town, and led him to the brow of the hill on which their town was built, so that they might hurl him off the cliff. 30 But he passed through the midst of them and went on his way.

How quickly the tide turned! Jesus went from being their best hope for a new future to being run out on a rail in the same breath. What happened? What went wrong? After saying all of these wonderful things, Jesus committed a terrible atrocity. Jesus pointed out that the kingdom of God was not just for the Jews. Jesus dared to say that God's kingdom extended outside of the chosen people, that God's grace was unlimited.

The people in Jesus' hometown were ready to accept grace and freedom—for themselves. They were ready to call him a prophet, to ride into fame on his coattails for the liberation of Israel. But when Jesus brought up the reality that God's grace extends beyond Israel, beyond themselves, they tried to shove him off a cliff! They could not accept that the freedom offered to them was offered to others outside of their group, so they missed out on it completely.

How do you feel about grace? Whom do you struggle to see as covered by, or offered, God's grace? In what ways do you try to draw lines around God's freedom and salvation for yourself? for others?

Workers Ahead

Surely our churches today are not guilty of the same kinds of actions! We would never seek to limit God's love and grace to people we know, those to whom we relate—people like us—would we? Unfortunately, such thoughts and actions are still very much a problem for would-be followers of the Christ. We divide along lines of denominations under the banner of "correct theology." We divide along lines of social stature. We divide along lines of race. There are times when it seems that much more divides us than unites us.

Read Luke 4:31-32.

He went down to Capernaum, a city in Galilee, and was teaching them on the Sabbath. ³² They were astounded at his teaching, because he spoke with authority.

Jesus couldn't do more for his hometown because he had a lack of power or ability, but because the people there were not open to him. So Jesus moved on to another place and another group where he taught with authority among them.

The freedom Jesus offers to us is sometimes so shocking that we can't bring ourselves to accept it. Lack of openness keeps us from really experiencing the life-giving grace God made available through Christ.

Imagine with me for a moment a large banquet table. This table is filled with people whom God has invited, whom God loves. Whom would you like to see there? Whom would you be upset to see seated next to you? It's not easy to admit, but each of us has drawn a line in our own heart. Some are not comfortable being around people who are homeless or those who are bouncing from home to home. Others would prefer to be seated with people of their own race or own nationality. Some would be horrified if the person next to them had tattoos. Some would rather do anything than sit next to a banker or CEO. But God's kingdom is bigger than all of our issues and fears. God calls on the church to reflect and embody the love shared with the world.

How has God's grace shocked you? your faith community? Where have you shut the door to God's grace? In what ways are you reaching out past your comfort zone?

How are you individually, and as a faith community, working to make your faith community look more like the kingdom of God? Do you intentionally reach out beyond yourselves? What does, or should this, look like? What steps do you need to take to lead towards more inclusion?

In the Rear View

As a group, pray for God's leading as you try to reflect God's love to all corners of the earth. How much more would God be able to do with followers who are willing to reach beyond their self-made constraints into the hurting, needing world?

Travel Log

Day 1:

    Take a moment today and revert to childhood. Find some pictures, either online or in magazines or newspapers, and make a collage of faces. These faces should represent the kingdom of God. Be sure to include people who might make you uncomfortable. Use this image this week as you pray and study to remind yourself that God's grace is wider and deeper than just you and your community.

Day 2:

    Jesus was not able to serve in his hometown because of the people's fear and anger. Where are you experiencing fear? anger? Are you open to God's presence in these situations, or are you keeping God out? Ask God to tear down any barriers you have created that keep Jesus from working through and in you. Draw a simple picture to represent your fears and anger. Add a second frame to show how it would change if you were to remove the barriers.

Day 3:

Who are those in need of liberation in your community? Write down names or groups as they come to mind. Pray for each of these individuals or groups today. Ask God to show you how you can help them and how you can show them God's grace today.

Day 4:

The Cumberland Presbyterian Church has begun work in Central America as a new mission field. Write a prayer for these efforts and the people who are involved.

Day 5:

The church universal is divided over many issues. Throughout the centuries, these differences have led to wars, bloodshed between families, and scars that may not heal in our lifetime. In what areas of division do you or your faith community participate? Where do you actively seek unity? List at least three ways that you can promote the unity of the church.

Day 6:

Jesus went on to other regions and found them much more receptive to his teachings than his hometown. What regions of your life are currently open to God's actions? Where do you notice God working in and through you? Jot down some of those below.

As you continue on the Lenten journey to the cross and Resurrection, think about places in your life where you need a resurrection. Ask God to help you find new life through Christ's teachings.

Day 7:

Spend some time looking at the collage you made on day one. Do the faces that made you uncomfortable still bother you as much? Do you still have the same reaction to the pictures? Are there perhaps others you need to add? Write down your feelings; revisit them closer to Easter.

God is continually at work in and through us. Thank God today for the liberation offered to you and others.

The Last Meal

Scripture for lesson:
Luke 22:7-23

What's the first thing that comes to mind when you think of the Last Supper? Where do these thoughts originate?

Prep for the Journey

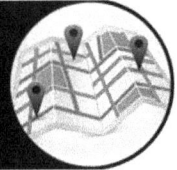

When we think of the Last Supper, many of us picture the famous painting by Leonardo da Vinci. You know the one, with Jesus and his disciples all crowded on one side of the table like they have been asked to move so they can all fit in the frame. Like it or not, this image has affected the way we view the Last Supper, not only in our imaginations, but also in our theology.

On the Road

Luke's description of the Last Supper is a very unique account. It begins with the revelation that the chief priest and teachers of the law are looking for ways to get rid of Jesus. They had gone so far as to bribe a member of Christ's inner circle, Judas, to help with their efforts. The whole thing is very dark and mysterious, and has an air of suspense.

In verse seven we learn that the preparations for Passover were at hand. Jesus sent out disciples to make sure a place was ready.

Read Luke 22:7-13.

Then came the day of Unleavened Bread, on which the Passover lamb had to be sacrificed. [8] So Jesus sent Peter and John, saying, "Go and prepare the Passover meal for us that we may eat it." [9] They asked

him, "Where do you want us to make preparations for it?" [10] "Listen,"
he said to them, "when you have entered the city, a man carrying a jar
of water will meet you; follow him into the house he enters [11] and say to
the owner of the house, 'The teacher asks you, "Where is the guest room,
where I may eat the Passover with my disciples?"' [12] He will show you a
large room upstairs, already furnished. Make preparations for us there."
[13] So they went and found everything as he had told them; and they
prepared the Passover meal.

At first glance this passage may not seem important or even
unusual to us. Jesus said that it was time for the Passover meal, and
his followers asked where they were to observe it. Jesus told them,
and they went to make preparations. No big deal. However, when we
begin to look at this passage closely, we can see some unique factors.

The Passover is one of the oldest and most important religious
celebrations in Judaism. It was one of the three "pilgrimage festivals"
for which all of the people in Judah traveled to Jerusalem so that they
could offer sacrifices at the Temple. Passover commemorates the
escape of the Hebrew slaves from Egypt. By spreading the blood of a
lamb on the doorposts, as God instructed, the firstborn sons of the
Hebrew people were spared from the last plague because the angel of
death "passed over" their houses.

It's likely that Jesus and his disciples had celebrated the Passover
together before, especially since this feast is observed in "family"
units. Since Jerusalem would have been inundated with visitors, the
disciples would have needed to know where they would gather for
this special meal. All of the preparations for the feast had to be made
before sundown, when the Sabbath began.

Jesus told the disciples to look for a man carrying water. In those
days, carrying water was mainly considered to be a woman's job. A
man carrying water would have stood out like a sore thumb. It sounds
like a one-in-a-million occurrence. However, since Jesus said that the
man would "meet" the disciples, it sounds as if he had already made
these plans. The disciples could not risk going into the house of an
unknown person or innkeeper with Jesus along. His life was being
threatened, so the need for security would have been paramount.

Scenic Route

The hour for the meal arrived and Jesus rejoiced with his disciples, telling them how much he had wanted to share this meal with
them. It should have been a great and happy time. Jesus had entered
Jerusalem in triumph to shouts of "Hosanna!" People had proclaimed
him as the Messiah, the King. Amidst all of this bustling excitement,
you can feel the anticipation. But Jesus' words didn't seem to match
the hype.

What, if any, religious festivals
are important to you or your
church community? How do
you handle preparations? What
is left to chance?

How does the idea of advance
preparation affect the way you
see the Last Supper?

How do you react to the idea of Jesus suffering? How do you think the disciples reacted?

Read Luke 22:14-18.

When the hour came, he [Jesus] took his place at the table, and the apostles with him. [15] *He said to them, "I have eagerly desired to eat this Passover with you before I suffer;* [16] *for I tell you, I will not eat it until it is fulfilled in the kingdom of God."* [17] *Then he took a cup, and after giving thanks he said, "Take this and divide it among yourselves;* [18] *for I tell you that from now on I will not drink of the fruit of the vine until the kingdom of God comes."*

Excuse me, Jesus, did you say "suffer"? That word seems out of place with the idea of a king coming to claim his rightful throne. That kind of talk is for others, not the Son of God. Yet Jesus was clear: he would suffer, and soon.

In the next two verses, we find what we have come to know as the words of institution. These words, or a version thereof, are used by almost all denominations every time the Lord's Supper is celebrated.

Read Luke 22:19-20.

Then he took a loaf of bread, and when he had given thanks, he broke it and gave it to them, saying, "This is my body, which is given for you. Do this in remembrance of me." [20] *And he did the same with the cup after supper, saying, "This cup that is poured out for you is the new covenant in my blood."*

These words have been interpreted many different ways over the generations. In fact, I would dare to say that the members of your study group have different interpretations of them. Despite the differences, Christians around the world still participate in the remembering act of Communion. This observance is an opportunity to make Christ's death and resurrection real again. It is a chance to glimpse the kingdom of God together. It is an act of remembering what Jesus did for us.

Workers Ahead   CAUTION

But this meal did not end with these words, at least not according to Luke.

Read Luke 22: 21-23.

But see, the one who betrays me is with me, and his hand is on the table. [22] *For the Son of Man is going as it has been determined, but woe to that one by whom he is betrayed!"* [23] *Then they began to ask one another which one of them it could be who would do this.*

Talk about a dramatic shift! We go from the words that we have treasured and turned into a vital part of our worship to these words from Jesus: "Woe to that one by whom he is betrayed!" We, who have heard the story, who know the ending, realize of course that he was speaking of Judas. For the disciples, their confusion at Jesus' words of suffering turned into shock that betrayal would come from one of their own. We can picture Judas squirming in his seat, sweat forming on his brow. But it's important to note that the disciples did not have this reaction. They began to ask one another who would do this. They realized what we so often forget: any one of us is capable of betraying Christ.

In fact, we do it almost every day. Not one of us lives a life void of sin. There are moments when we turn away from Jesus, when we deny Jesus, and even when we betray Jesus. These are not things we like to admit, or even acknowledge, but that doesn't mean they don't happen.

In the Rear View

Those closest to Jesus, who saw him on a daily basis and sat at his feet to learn, questioned if they were capable of betraying Christ. This is something with which we deal even today. However, we deal with it in light of the death and resurrection of Jesus. We are blessed to know the rest of the story. We know that Jesus is the promised Messiah, the culmination of hundreds of years of prophecy. We know that Jesus has forgiven sin—past, present, and future. We can rest assured that our debt has been paid.

So what do we do with that knowledge? How do we share these truths? One way is by taking time to remember this story. Take time to read this account together and remember that the gift of reconciliation was offered to all—even Judas, the betrayer of the Christ; even all the other disciples who wondered if they were betrayer of whom Jesus spoke; and even to us who know the ending and still fall to temptation daily.

Take a moment and think of ways that you have betrayed Christ. How can you strive to be more authentic to Christ daily?

If it is available and your group desires to do so, join in the celebration of Communion to end this lesson. Or, share other signs of remembrance or reconciliation with one another.

Travel Log

Day 1:

Jesus had apparently made arrangements for a place where he and his disciples could gather to worship and spend time together. Do you think he still does so today? How often do you set aside and plan time to spend with him? with other disciples? Plan at least one time this week, in addition to Sunday morning, to set aside time for God. Make some notes about how you will prepare for that time.

Day 2:

Jesus said that he eagerly desired to spend time with the disciples, which denotes their importance to him. They had been his supporters and friends throughout his ministry. How do you feel about Jesus eagerly desiring to spend time with you? How can you be more open to acknowledging Christ's presence in your life? in the world? List at least three ways.

Day 3:

The words of Institution found in verses 19-20 are very special in most congregations. What do you think of when you read or hear those words? How do they make you feel? Are those words fresh when you hear them, or do they seem more like an old habit? How does ritual affect the way you view your relationship with God? with the church? Journal your thoughts below.

Day 4:

The act of sharing a meal together was an important custom in Jesus' time. Those with whom one chose to associate and dine said a lot about the person's character and goals. Jesus was excited about dining with a tax collector, fishermen, and other questionable characters. Jesus cares not for titles and power, but for people.

To whom do you give your time? With whom do you get excited about spending time? List those people below. Take a moment this week and plan a meal that will include those people who are important to you. Let them know their importance to you by focusing your attention on them.

Day 5:

How often does your community of faith celebrate Communion? How do you prepare for these times? If there are things that you feel would help you to be better prepared for the next time Communion is served, note them below.

Day 6:

We've thought a lot about our importance to Jesus and his importance to us. Read Psalm 23 with those thoughts in mind. Write down things that stand out to you about this psalm as you consider it from the perspective of Jesus making advance preparations for the Last Supper. How do those preparations translate to the sacrament being available to us?

Day 7:

Jesus gathered his loved ones to him because he knew that his death was near. If today were your last opportunity to share your love and thoughts with those closest to you, what might you say? What might you do? What keeps you from sharing those feelings and thoughts now? Make some notes about what you want to tell people. Follow up by calling or writing to them soon.

Restless Times

FAITH LIFE

Scripture for lesson:
Luke 22:39-53

What things help to calm and comfort you? How often do you do them?

Prep for the Journey

When the world becomes overwhelming, I like to find a quiet place to rest. Sometimes I read, sometimes I knit, and often I pray. These things help me to find my way from panic to peace.

On the Road

This scripture takes place after the Last Supper. Jesus had said some strange things, and the disciples were confused as to what might happen next.

Read Luke 22: 39-42.

He came out and went, as was his custom, to the Mount of Olives; and the disciples followed him. 40 When he reached the place, he said to them, "Pray that you may not come into the time of trial." 41 Then he withdrew from them about a stone's throw, knelt down, and prayed, 42 "Father, if you are willing, remove this cup from me; yet, not my will but yours be done."

The Mount of Olives is a ridge east of Jerusalem that was once covered with olive trees. Both Jesus and the disciples would have been familiar with this area as it was necessary to cross the mount to go from Jerusalem to Bethany. Jesus would also have gone down the mount as he entered Jerusalem on Palm Sunday. It is likely that Jesus and the disciples camped in the garden at various times, as it was known to be a place where travelers stayed, especially during times of pilgrimages when the city would have been overflowing with visitors.

What does the phrase "follow me" mean to you? What promises do you hear in those words?

Although Luke does not say that Jesus went to the Garden of Gethsemane, as do other Gospel accounts, Gethsemane is near the foot of the Mount of Olives. Gardens were places where people went to escape the heat of the day, to enjoy the beauty of plants, and to find solitude. Jesus frequently went to this area to pray. The disciples followed him. They had been called throughout their time with Christ to follow him, and this occasion was no different.

The disciples faithfully followed Jesus on what would become the most difficult journey they had encountered. Those who know the story know that this trip would lead to death and suffering. Following Jesus does not mean that things will be all sunshine and roses. Following Jesus can have very real, very painful consequences.

Jesus hadn't called the disciples away for one last hurrah or a bonfire where they could reminisce. He called them away to pray.

Prayer is a major theme in Luke's Gospel. It tells of many times when Jesus went away to pray. Jesus taught the disciples how to pray. Jesus' prayers were powerful and life-changing.

When they reached the Mount of Olives, Jesus told the disciples to pray so that they would not come into the time of trial. He was encouraging them to use the best of all preparations for the time ahead. Jesus knew that the next several hours would be intense, and that without adequate preparation the disciples would falter and fall.

Luke gives us a glimpse into Jesus' personal prayers: "Father, if you are willing, remove this cup from me; yet, not my will but yours be done." Jesus was perhaps more human in this moment than in any other. He would rather not have been a martyr. He would rather not have had to suffer pain and death. Yet he turned his life over completely to the will of God. In this moment we see Jesus taking up the mantle laid before him and rising to greet what would come.

Scenic Route

Prayer is more than just a brief conversation with God when you are in need. Prayer is a way of life, a way of creating and maintaining a relationship with God.

Read Luke 22: 43-44.

Then an angel from heaven appeared to him and gave him strength.
⁴⁴ In his anguish he prayed more earnestly, and his sweat became like great drops of blood falling down on the ground.

Jesus was in deep anguish and pain during this prayer time. While we only have one line from the prayer, tradition tells us that this was a deep, soul-searching moment for him. This passage is not in all of the ancient manuscripts, and there is a tendency to overlook it for

What consequences are you ready to face in following Jesus? For what consequences are you ill prepared?

When have you felt strengthened or renewed by time spent in prayer? How does prayer change things?

What does comfort in times of grief and suffering mean to you? How have you received God's comfort?

Is there a time in your life when you might have handled things differently if you had been spiritually prepared? What are you doing now to maintain a healthy spiritual life?

that reason. However, we can learn about Christ's character and God's attitude through these verses. A heavenly messenger was sent to bring Christ strength. Even while his sweat was pouring out of him like blood (not as blood, but like blood), he was receiving comfort from God.

After this time of raw exposure and being strengthened, Jesus returned to his disciples. He was not pleased with how he found them.

Read Luke 22:45-46.

When he got up from prayer, he came to the disciples and found them sleeping because of grief, ⁴⁶ and he said to them, "Why are you sleeping? Get up and pray that you may not come into the time of trial."

Jesus returned from his time of prayer to find his disciples asleep rather than praying. He woke them with words of rebuke: Why are you not praying! Jesus had given them specific instructions, which they did not follow.

In the disciples' defense, going to the Mount of Olives likely meant returning to where they were camped. We all know how difficult it can be to stay awake when we return "home" after a long day, especially with a full stomach.

Knowing that trouble had been brewing, the disciples had tried to prepare themselves for the showdown that was obviously coming. Some were even prepared to defend themselves and Jesus with weapons. However, they were not prepared to defend themselves spiritually. They did not yet understand Jesus' role as Messiah and were not prepared for what would happen next.

As Jesus was speaking to the disciples, a crowd came. This crowd was different from all of the other crowds of people who had followed Jesus. This crowd came at night and seemed menacing; it was led by Judas.

Read Luke 22:47-51.

While he was still speaking, suddenly a crowd came, and the one called Judas, one of the twelve, was leading them. He approached Jesus to kiss him; ⁴⁸ but Jesus said to him, "Judas, is it with a kiss that you are betraying the Son of Man?" ⁴⁹ When those who were around him saw what was coming, they asked, "Lord, should we strike with the sword?" ⁵⁰ Then one of them struck the slave of the high priest and cut off his right ear. ⁵¹ But Jesus said, "No more of this!" And he touched his ear and healed him.

Luke had not previously given any indication of Judas having exited the group. But Judas brought a mob of angry, armed men. Instantly we are reminded of Jesus' words during the Last Supper, "One of you will betray me." Judas, the betrayer, had come.

Imagine the emotional swing the disciples would have experienced. Standing before them was one of their own who had brought an angry mob to take Jesus away. They took his betrayal very personally. Judas' motives didn't matter; his name remains tainted.

Judas greeted Jesus with a kiss, which was sometimes used to show reverence to the Lord. However, Jesus made sure everyone was aware that Judas' kiss was not a friendly or reverent act. The disciples knew that Jesus had not orchestrated the arrival of Judas and the angry crowd, which caused them to react defensively. They wondered, *Should we strike with the sword? Should we attack? Should we defend? What is the right course of action?*

An unnamed disciple struck the high priest's servant, cutting off his right ear. This act of violence should have been the start of a bloody battle, or perhaps even the start of a revolution. However, Jesus stopped it all with his reaction, "No more of this!" He then reached out and healed the servant's ear. In the midst of his own suffering, Jesus still acted to heal.

Workers Ahead

Jesus rejected violence as the way to accomplish God's goals. Even though there were armed men ready to die for him, Jesus said, "No more!" This statement doesn't sound like the conquering hero the people had praised a few days earlier when Jesus had entered Jerusalem. These events are troubling to us. This action of peace, when he could have resisted, does not agree with our idea of what victory looks like. We like winners, people who overcome insurmountable odds to rise to the top. But Jesus told the disciples to put away their swords, and he walked into the hands of the enemy.

God's ways are not our ways. Where we see weakness and frailty, God sees strength and wholeness. Living these ideals in a world that celebrates power and strength through oppression is not easy. There will be hard and painful choices. And that's where turning to God continually in prayer and praise will help us toward our goal. The ways of the world are not always as good as they seem.

Read Luke 22:52-53.

Then Jesus said to the chief priests, the officers of the temple police, and the elders who had come for him, "Have you come out with swords and clubs as if I were a bandit? [53] When I was with you day after day in the temple, you did not lay hands on me. But this is your hour, and the power of darkness!"

Those in power struggled with Jesus' messages because he offered things that went against the corrupt power system. Jesus' teachings offered nothing less than freedom and life. The lost are saved, given new life by the death of Christ.

When have you asked Jesus for the right way to respond in a situation? Did you wait for his answer or strike out on your own?

How do you respond to Jesus' actions on the Mount of Olives? What message did he send?

Brainstorm ways you and your faith community can show others the freedom and new life you have received in Christ. How have you personally been doing these things?

Write your name on a slip of paper. Compile all the names. Each person will draw a name. For the remainder of Lent, pray for the person whose name you drew.

In the Rear View

The moments leading up to the trial and crucifixion of Christ were not pretty. There is nothing we can or should do to romanticize or white wash them. There is much to be learned from Jesus' suffering and his preparation for that suffering.

Day 1:

Focus on the person whose name you drew. Pray for any needs in his or her life of which you are aware. Write the person's name down in the space below. Pray for something that begins with each letter of his or her first name. For example: Jane might be joy, abundance, nurture, emotional support.

Day 2:

It was not God's will to remove the cup of suffering from Jesus. Does this mean that God did not hear Jesus' prayer? When have you felt as if God did not hear your prayers? How did you react? What is your attitude towards prayer now? In the space below, write down some ways you can enhance your prayer life.

Day 3:

The disciples fell asleep while they were waiting on Jesus to return. When have you "fallen asleep" when waiting on God's actions? What have you learned from these experiences? List ways you can stay awake and alert for Christ.

Day 4:

Touch can harm or heal. Judas betrayed Jesus with a kiss, a touch usually associated with care. But in this case, a kiss stood for betrayal. Jesus, on the other hand, touched the servant's ear and healed the man. In what ways have you been harmed by others? How have you experienced healing from others? What can you do to try to ensure that your touch is healing? Journal about the ways you have given healing touches and places where you could have been more healing.

Day 5:

What bothers you about the scripture used in this lesson? What comforts you? What questions do you have about what occurred? While talking with someone else about these questions, write down any insights you gain or questions that arise. Pray about them, asking God to clarify things for you.

Day 6:

Throughout history people have used the name of Jesus to commit terrible atrocities, which still happens today. How do we as Christians handle others using Jesus as an excuse for violence or hate? How do we react? How should we react? Write down situations where people are misusing Jesus as a reason for such actions. Pray for these situations.

Day 7:

    Lent is a time for reflection. What have you learned about yourself during this Lenten study? What have you learned about God? How will these things change the way you interact with God or others? Record your reflections.

The Mocked Messiah

Scripture for lesson:
Luke 23:26-56

Prep for the Journey

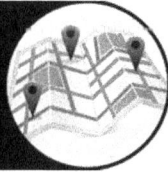

I have a large birthmark on the left side of the back of my neck. As I've grown it has faded a bit, but as a child it was the source of constant ridicule. Sixth grade was a merciless time of taunting from all corners. Some said it was something you could catch, others said it was a hickey, and still others said it was some weird, alien growth. I realize now that several kids were made fun of for little things, but at the time, I thought I was the only one and that the mocking would never end.

On the Road

Chapter 23 of Luke tells us perhaps the most difficult story in all of scripture: the account of the trial and crucifixion of Jesus. The events of what would later come to be called Holy Week led up to these moments.

After having been tried and found guilty, Jesus was sentenced to death by crucifixion. The leaders who wanted him out of the way took Jesus to Pilate, the Roman-appointed governor of Judea, because the Jews did not have the authority to impose the death penalty.

Crucifixion was a horrible method of execution. After having been sentenced, the criminal was beaten with a whip made of thongs that had pieces of metal or bone attached to the ends. The beating was meant to hasten death.

After the beating, the criminal was forced to carry the crossbeam to the site of the execution, which was intended to break the person's

When have you been mocked? How did it feel?

Who has come from the crowd to help you? How did the experience affect you?

With what things in your life are you struggling? What things do you see ahead for which Jesus may be preparing you? How should you prepare to face the challenges ahead, knowing that with God you will not be standing against them alone?

will to live. Jesus was so weaken that he could not carry the crossbeam. The soldiers pulled a stranger from the crowd and forced him to carry the cross for Jesus.

Read Luke 23:26-31.

As they led him away, they seized a man, Simon of Cyrene, who was coming from the country, and they laid the cross on him, and made him carry it behind Jesus. [27] *A great number of the people followed him, and among them were women who were beating their breasts and wailing for him.* [28] *But Jesus turned to them and said, "Daughters of Jerusalem, do not weep for me, but weep for yourselves and for your children.* [29] *For the days are surely coming when they will say, 'Blessed are the barren, and the wombs that never bore, and the breasts that never nursed.'* [30] *Then they will begin to say to the mountains, 'Fall on us'; and to the hills, 'Cover us.'* [31] *For if they do this when the wood is green, what will happen when it is dry?"*

This passage speaks of Jesus talking with the women who mourned him on his way to the cross. Jesus' words were less than comforting: "Cry for yourselves, not for me." Jesus knew that his journey would not end at the cross or even at the tomb. He also knew that these women would be facing quite a struggle in the months and years to come.

Jesus had affirmed time and time again that he was the Messiah, yet in his last moments he was faced once more with questions of his identity. However, this time they took on the bitter tone of mockery.

Read Luke 23:32-39.

Two others also, who were criminals, were led away to be put to death with him. [33] *When they came to the place that is called The Skull, they crucified Jesus there with the criminals, one on his right and one on his left. [[*[34] *Then Jesus said, "Father, forgive them; for they do not know what they are doing."]] And they cast lots to divide his clothing.* [35] *And the people stood by, watching; but the leaders scoffed at him, saying, "He saved others; let him save himself if he is the Messiah of God, his chosen one!"* [36] *The soldiers also mocked him, coming up and offering him sour wine,* [37] *and saying, "If you are the King of the Jews, save yourself!"* [38] *There was also an inscription over him, "This is the King of the Jews."*

[39] *One of the criminals who were hanged there kept deriding him and saying, "Are you not the Messiah? Save yourself and us!"*

It is hard to imagine a setting less royal, less sovereign, than that of a cross at Golgotha. Yet this is where we find the Savior and King of the world. The soldiers had cast lots for his clothing, a common practice. Those gathered around waited to see what would happen. The leaders were the ones who spoke, perhaps emboldened by the fact that Jesus no longer seemed to be a threat. They cried out, "Let him save himself, if he is who he claims to be."

Isn't that just like the leaders of the world? They do everything they can to squash anyone or anything that might threaten their power; when they think they have succeeded, they can't help but gloat.

The soldiers joined in the fun, calling out to him to save himself. They even went so far as to place a sign over his head that stated: "This is the king of the Jews." The public humiliation was so strong that the thief next to Jesus derided him as well. Such treatment placed Christ lower even than that thief.

Christ died much like how he was born—weak, rejected, exposed, and vulnerable. Finding ourselves in a vulnerable position often exposes our true selves. Sometimes that exposure teaches us things about ourselves we'd rather not know, things we'd rather not think about. Sometimes it shows us for whom we really care or what we are really capable of doing. It is in this vulnerability, this point of weakness, that Jesus' true self was shown. For some, it was the first time they were able to see him for who he really was.

Read Luke 23:40-43.

But the other rebuked him, saying, "Do you not fear God, since you are under the same sentence of condemnation? 41 And we indeed have been condemned justly, for we are getting what we deserve for our deeds, but this man has done nothing wrong." 42 Then he said, "Jesus, remember me when you come into your kingdom." 43 He replied, "Truly I tell you, today you will be with me in Paradise."

Just like the witness of the shepherds and wise men who came to honor Jesus at birth, Jesus had a witness to honor him in death. True, this witness is a criminal, but the shepherds were not much more highly regarded. This unnamed, dying criminal confessed to knowing who Jesus was and asked to be remembered, to be regarded when Jesus came into his kingdom. And Jesus, who was going through more agony than we can imagine, replied with words of hope: "Today you will be with me in paradise."

Scenic Route

Throughout the church's history, this passage has been used to justify what are called "deathbed conversions." If the thief on the cross could enter heaven, any of us can as long as we confess our belief in Christ as the Messiah before our dying breath. Many people have found great comfort in this notion. Many people have delayed making a faith commitment because of the hope found in this kind of last-minute opportunity.

This passage is not about how lucky the penitent criminal was, but about the absolute authority and mercy of Jesus. True, it highlights for us the reality that our deeds cannot save us; only Christ can do that. However, at its heart, it shows Jesus's kingship by revealing his commitment to redeem human life regardless of the situation, condition,

> When have you witnessed people mocking Jesus? his followers? When have you participated in such mockery?

> How do you as a community of faith feel about "deathbed conversions"? Why? What else do you gather from these verses?

or timing. Even on the very instrument of his death, Jesus brought new life!

By welcoming the criminal into the kingdom, Jesus extended mercy beyond the boundaries we would seek to place. Not only did Jesus welcome this man into community, he also uttered words of forgiveness for others. On the cross, Jesus did what we find so hard to do, even impossible to do: forgive those who wound us most deeply.

Read again Luke 23:34.

Then Jesus said, "Father, forgive them; for they do not know what they are doing."

Jesus forgives those who, to us, seem to deserve it the least—those actively committing evil, those who don't believe and are unrepentant. Jesus offers them a gift they don't even recognize—radical forgiveness. This forgiveness, so in line with his teachings, is sometimes hard for us to recognize as well.

These words of forgiveness are not just for the people who stood by and watched Jesus be crucified. They are not just for the soldiers who followed heinous orders or mocked Jesus. They are not only for the political or religious leaders of that time. These are words for everyone, for all time. "Father, forgive them; for they do not know what they are doing." We are not always aware of the harm our sin causes ourselves or others. We are not always alert to the ways in which our action or inaction may be putting Christ in a bad light. Yet, Christ petitions on our behalf for our forgiveness.

Read Luke 23:44-49.

It was now about noon, and darkness came over the whole land until three in the afternoon, [45] while the sun's light failed; and the curtain of the temple was torn in two. [46] Then Jesus, crying with a loud voice, said, "Father, into your hands I commend my spirit." Having said this, he breathed his last. [47] When the centurion saw what had taken place, he praised God and said, "Certainly this man was innocent." [48] And when all the crowds who had gathered there for this spectacle saw what had taken place, they returned home, beating their breasts. [49] But all his acquaintances, including the women who had followed him from Galilee, stood at a distance, watching these things.

Imagine yourself as part of the crowd who had gathered. It's likely that a mob mentality existed as Jesus was beaten and hung on the cross. Some of those people were Jesus' followers; others may have been visiting the city and just wanted to see what all of the excitement was about. It reminds me of hangings in the Old West of the United States. People came from miles around to attend a hanging. They brought a picnic meal and turned it into a social event.

People in Jesus' time were very superstitious. Just imagine how scared they must have been when the sun's light failed. Some people attribute the midday darkness to an eclipse; however, Passover (which had just been celebrated) occurred when the moon was full, thus making an eclipse impossible. Then to find that the curtain between

In what ways do you struggle to forgive? How does your community of faith handle forgiveness? Are there issues of forgiveness with which you or your community of faith need to deal?

When have you experienced "mob mentality"? How did you feel during that time? afterward?

How do you feel when people use scientific explanations for biblical occurrences?

48

the holy of holies and the holy place in the Temple, which was made from one piece of cloth, had been torn in half added to their fear. These events so affected people that they left remorseful.

Death by crucifixion could take several days and was ultimately caused by loss of blood circulation. The body remained on the cross even after death as it rotted and became food for scavenging birds, a further degradation of the corpse. Unlike most of those who were crucified, Jesus had friends who removed his body and placed it in a tomb.

Read Luke 23:50-56.

Now there was a good and righteous man named Joseph, who, though a member of the council, [51] had not agreed to their plan and action. He came from the Jewish town of Arimathea, and he was waiting expectantly for the kingdom of God. [52] This man went to Pilate and asked for the body of Jesus. [53] Then he took it down, wrapped it in a linen cloth, and laid it in a rock-hewn tomb where no one had ever been laid. [54] It was the day of Preparation, and the sabbath was beginning. [55] The women who had come with him from Galilee followed, and they saw the tomb and how his body was laid. [56] Then they returned, and prepared spices and ointments.

On the sabbath they rested according to the commandment.

Workers Ahead

On the last day of his life, indeed when death came, the religious authorities and the Roman authorities hoped they were through with this rabble-rouser, this blasphemer. However, Jesus' death and resurrection made clear that he was sovereign over all creation. I can't imagine a better king than one who, until the very end of his human life, was looking for ways to heal and restore the world. Since we know he was doing this from the cross, imagine what he is doing even now!

Many people live in communities that are deeply divided over issues that occurred in the past. Perhaps these are instances of personal hurts. Perhaps they are pains caused by systematic racism or sexism. Perhaps they are scars from wars long since ended. Unless we deal with these scars, it will be next to impossible to end these divisions and seek the healing that only forgiveness and reconciliation can offer.

As Christ's followers, we should extend forgiveness and new life to the world in which we find ourselves, which is not always easy to do. It is often much simpler to hold onto our resentments or to ignore them completely. However, if Christ found it possible to forgive those who put him to death, we should be able to forgive those who have harmed us.

How can you as a community of faith extend Christ's forgiveness? Onto what is the community of faith holding that might be keeping them from experiencing new life?

49

In the Rear View

We may have been mocked in our past. We may have been unjustly vilified by our peers. We may have been treated as less than human. These things hurt, they scar, and they can lead to all sorts of problems. Too often, that's just what we let them do—become things that destroy us, that tear down our lives. If we believe what we confess, that Jesus' salvation, forgiveness, and reconciliation are for all, then who are we to withhold any of it from others?

Pray together for forgiveness of your own shortcomings and sins, but also for the strength to begin the process of forgiving others. Pray that God will bring about forgiveness in the hearts of your community of faith and throughout the body of Christ worldwide. Pray that God's forgiveness and new life will spread beyond your sphere of influence into the whole of creation, that all who have breath may praise the Lord!

Day 1:

   Jesus was falsely accused and convicted. The common people comprised the overwhelming majority of Jesus' followers, but they either didn't try or were unable to stop the proceedings that led to his death. Of what situations are you aware when someone was falsely accused? What did you do on that person's behalf? How do you advocate for those who are being treated unjustly? Make a list of situations in your community that are unjust. Then list ways you can address those injustices.

Day 2:

   Simon from Cyrene was compelled to come alongside Jesus in his journey to Golgotha. What do you think that experience was like for him? Jesus was provided with a companion to the cross. The Holy Spirit is a willing companion who is with us every day. How does your vision of your daily life change when you picture the Holy Spirit helping you to carry your burdens? Jot down some times when you felt the Holy Spirit's presence in your daily life.

Day 3:

Forgiveness is not an easy thing. There are times when forgiving is the last thing we want to do. What or whom do you need to forgive? Write down these things or people and begin the process of forgiveness through prayer and, when possible and appropriate, contact with those involved.

Day 4:

Darkness covered the earth for three hours in the middle of the afternoon. It seems as if even creation mourned Jesus' death. The curtain of the Temple was torn in half during this time, which some scholars suggest signifies that there is no longer a divide between God and people. What in your life reflects that Jesus is Lord? What divisions have you put up between yourself and God? How can you begin to let God remove those divisions? As you reflect on these question, make some notes about them in the space below.

Day 5:

What evidence of God have you experienced? Where have you seen God acting? heard God speaking? felt God moving? Write down your thoughts and feelings about these experiences.

What made you aware of them? What made them memorable? How can you share your experiences or what you have learned from them with someone else?

Day 6:

After Jesus' death, the centurion who had overseen the proceedings praised God and acknowledged Jesus as the Son of God. Why do you think he was able to make this claim? What is it about Jesus that lets you claim his lordship? What in your life allows others to see that you have the faith to proclaim Jesus as Lord? Jot down some ideas as to how you will show your faith to others.

Day 7:

    Jesus was laid to rest in a tomb. There was no pomp and circumstance, no pretty words were said. This ending was not what one have would expected. But the reader is given hope. The women watched where he was laid. They then returned home to prepare spices and perfumes to use on his body after their observance of the Sabbath. Their preparations give us hope that there is more to come. What preparations are you making in your life to let people know that the crucifixion is not the end of Jesus' story? Write down some additional preparations you think would be helpful.

Resurrection:
An Idle Tale

Scripture for lesson:
Luke 24:1-12

Prep for the Journey

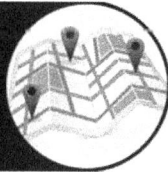

I often wonder what life was like for the followers of Jesus who lived through what we call Holy Week. I try to imagine what I might have felt after a week that had started with shouts of Hosanna, turned into demands to crucify, and ended with tears of grief.

On the Road

After an emotional week during which their friend and teacher was executed like a common criminal, Jesus' followers had to have wondered what they were going to do next. What would they do now that their leader was gone? Where would they go? What were they supposed to do now that their very purpose in life lay dead in a tomb?

Read Luke 24:1.
But on the first day of the week, at early dawn, they came to the tomb, taking the spices that they had prepared.
When the women left for the tomb on that first Easter morning, they knew what awaited them, or so they thought. Since Jesus had died just before the beginning of the Sabbath, the observance of which began at sundown, there had not been time to prepare his body for burial. Intending to do so after the Sabbath, these women took the appropriate spices and left for the tomb where his body had been placed, expecting to find the tomb just as they had last seen it.

Those of us who are familiar with the Easter story already know what they found when they arrived at the tomb. In our minds, they

How might you have felt as a follower of Christ after those events?

What might you be thinking if you were walking with the women that first Easter morning?

Share how you felt or reacted the first time the Resurrection became more than just a story to you.

were headed for the empty tomb, which symbolizes the glory of God's redemptive power and eternal life. But we have to remember that the women were expecting to gaze upon, and touch, death. They brought the things necessary to prepare their loved one for an everlasting sleep—not everlasting life.

Read Luke 24:2-9.

They found the stone rolled away from the tomb, ³ but when they went in, they did not find the body. ⁴ While they were perplexed about this, suddenly two men in dazzling clothes stood beside them. ⁵ The women were terrified and bowed their faces to the ground, but the men said to them, "Why do you look for the living among the dead? He is not here, but has risen. ⁶ Remember how he told you, while he was still in Galilee, ⁷ that the Son of Man must be handed over to sinners, and be crucified, and on the third day rise again." ⁸ Then they remembered his words, ⁹ and returning from the tomb, they told all this to the eleven and to all the rest.

The women came expecting death, but when they arrived at the tomb, a surprise awaited them. As they got close enough to see the tomb, they saw that the stone that had blocked the entrance had been rolled away and Jesus' body was gone. Two men in dazzling garments appeared to them, frightening them. The men, whom most people consider to have been heavenly messengers (angels), said, "Why do you look for the living among the dead? Remember, he said he would die and on the third day rise again." Then they remembered and realized that Jesus had risen. So they ran to tell the others, "Jesus is alive!"

These women were mourning the death of Jesus when they had a sudden and completely unexpected encounter with the Resurrection. They came thinking that all was lost only to experience God's power in a place known for death. The resurrection invaded the place of the dead to bring good news of life. Some two thousand years later, the good news of Resurrection reshapes our notion of who Jesus is, and it is both unexpected and surprising.

Scenic Route

The women accepted the messengers' words at face value, but do you remember how the disciples reacted to the news of Jesus' resurrection?

Read Luke 24:8-12.

Now it was Mary Magdalene, Joanna, Mary the mother of James, and the other women with them who told this to the apostles. ¹¹ But these words seemed to them an idle tale, and they did not believe them. ¹² But Peter got up and ran to the tomb; stooping and looking in, he saw the linen cloths by themselves; then he went home, amazed at what had happened.

They didn't believe it. They thought it was an idle tale. However, Peter ran to see for himself. We don't know why Peter seems to have given the report some credence when the others did not. Perhaps he wanted to verify the report for himself. Maybe he so desperately wanted it to be true that he simply had to check it out personally rather than trust the report of others. After finding the burial cloths but not Jesus' body, Peter returned home. Just imagine the thoughts that must have been racing through his mind!

I have always wondered why they didn't accept this good news. It was good news, after all. The same could be asked of us today. Why will people accept bad news, even though they don't want to believe it, yet reject good news when they want to believe it? Getting news that a loved one who was once dead and now is alive is the kind of news that every mourning loved one wants to hear. But the disciples didn't believe the women when they told them. Their tale just seemed like a bad joke. After all, people just don't get up and walk out of their tombs.

Unfortunately, we are not that different from the disciples. We have a hard time understanding what happened that first Easter morning, and we have an even harder time accepting the new life that Jesus was offering.

Workers Ahead

Why is it that we fail to accept the new life that Christ is offering us? Perhaps it's because new life doesn't seem real. In this world, all we really know is death. Sometimes it is physical death, but often it is the death of our soul, the darkness of despair and the eternal loneliness of a poor self-image. We are so familiar with darkness that when someone promises a full and abundant life free from that which binds us, we dismiss their words as an idle tale of "religious fanatics."

The women went to the tomb to view death and were surprised to find life. I wonder what each of you were expecting to find when you came here today. Did you come to hear about a man who lived a good life and died a noble death? Perhaps you came because you thought you could learn something from such a man's life. Maybe you came because this is Easter and going to church is what a person does on Easter. Maybe you came because someone made you come.

Whatever the reason, I have some news for you! Jesus is alive! He has risen and is no longer in the tomb! This man who rose from the dead has the power to change our lives. The risen Christ can take the deadness of our life and transform it into new life. Jesus can take the broken pieces of our lives, resurrect them, and transform

What good news have you had trouble believing? What has enabled you to accept it?

57

them into something wonderful that is beyond our expectations and understanding. How do I know that Jesus can do this? Because he himself was once dead and he rose again. Through his resurrection he brought new life, not just to the women at the tomb, but to all who believe.

When we are open to letting God work in our lives, God can bring the unexpected surprise of resurrection.

In the Rear View

Hopefully, the good news has shocked us as it did the disciples so long ago. But how will we react to it? Will we write it off as an old wives' tale or idle talk? Will we go home like Peter, wondering about what we have seen and heard? Or will we run and tell others the good news that Jesus is alive and he wants to give new life to all?

Jesus has risen from the dead, and he offers us the chance to live with him. Believe in the Resurrection, not just as a historical incident, but also as a present, living reality. If we believe, the power of the Resurrection will change our lives. We will no longer be walking to the tombs, the place of the dead, as those women were. Instead we will be running, with the love of God filling our hearts. We will be running in joy, with the strength of new life. We will be running to tell others the good news.

Day 1:

Sadly, many people approach life with the same expectations that these women had when they first approached the tomb: Life is nothing more than a long walk toward death. Every day is another step closer to the tombs. Just as those women sorrowfully walked through the early morning mist, these people sadly walk through the midst of life. In what areas of your life are you just going through the motions? How do you need to be reminded of the power of new life given through Christ? Make some notes here about how you can remind yourself of the power of new life.

Day 2:

In what areas of your life do you expect death, but wish for a surprise? your work? your marriage? a hurt from your past? an addiction? This text is a reminder of how God's love and new life comes to us as a surprise. On the first Easter, God invaded this dead world with new life. God is still not done invading our dead lives with the good news of eternal life in Christ. Jot down ways in which God has invaded your life and brought new life. Thank God for these times, and ask God to show you where new life is being given in your current situations.

Day 3:

What areas of your community of faith need to be resurrected? How is God trying to bring new life into the community with which you worship and study? Pray for these areas and for the leaders of your congregation. Write down these prayers and refer to them frequently. Note when you see God moving or working with or through those areas or leaders.

Day 4:

There are times when we doubt. There are moments when we are convinced that the worst is ahead. At these times, we can really relate to the people in this scripture. They were scared, alone, and unsure. Journal about such times in your own life, including what helps you to get through them. Note the things you need to remember so that those times become less frequent.

Day 5:

When the women found the tomb empty, God's messengers told them that Jesus had risen and was alive. Who has shared the good news with you? Use the space below to write a note thanking those persons for their willingness to give God's words to you. If possible, share these words of thankfulness with the individuals. If not, consider with whom you might share those words to honor that special person.

Day 6:

In our world, resurrection can often seem like an idle tale. When we look around, we see empty strip malls, decaying buildings, failing systems, and aching hearts. Where do you see the need for resurrection in your community? How can you show others that resurrection is possible? Make notes as to how you will help others realize the promise of resurrection.

Day 7:

"Why do you seek the living among the dead? He has risen just as he said." Run to those you know and to the world to tell them, "Jesus is alive!" Make a list of people who need to hear this good news and then, go tell them! Call a friend who is in despair or in turmoil and share the good news of God's love and Christ's resurrection with him or her. Run like the women, and tell others that Christ lives and gives life. Christ is risen; he is risen indeed.

The Miracle of Hearing

Scripture for lesson:
Acts 2

Prep for the Journey

Many times the church doesn't seem to know what to do with the holy day of Pentecost. We know it was important; we call it the "birth-day of the church," but many of us struggle with what the implications of that day really are and how they apply to us today.

On the Road

The disciples were fresh from a forty-day period of intense study, renewal, and fellowship with the risen Lord. He walked with them, taught them, and prepared fish for them before ascending into heaven. As if that were not enough, Jesus promised his followers that God would send a comforter, a helper, to them so that they would never be alone in their faith.

Jesus told the disciples to remain in Jerusalem, where the memory of Jesus' crucifixion was still fresh in people's minds, and wait for this helper. Undoubtedly, anyone who was a known follower of Christ had a price on his or her head. The Roman government did not want, nor could they afford, an uprising. So these men and women of faith had to stay undercover for fear of losing their lives. They were all together in a house, probably preparing to celebrate the festival of weeks, when suddenly the house was filled with a rushing, violent wind.

What comes to mind when you think of Pentecost? What personal significance does Pentecost hold for you or your faith community?

Read Acts 2:1-4.

When the day of Pentecost had come, they were all together in one place. ² And suddenly from heaven there came a sound like the rush of a violent wind, and it filled the entire house where they were sitting. ³ Divided tongues, as of fire, appeared among them, and a tongue rested on each of them. ⁴ All of them were filled with the Holy Spirit and began to speak in other languages, as the Spirit gave them ability.

Can you imagine? A group of Christians who were all from the same geographical area, who spoke the same language and dialect, were suddenly speaking in languages from around the world! Some were speaking Arabic, others Greek, still others East Asian languages. Just think of the crowd's amazement!

Jerusalem was crowded with visitors from many different parts of the world as devout Jews gathered to celebrate Pentecost. Put yourself in the midst of the crowd. A violent wind sweeps across the city without warning. Then, from a nearby house, you hear people talking in many different languages—and they aren't being quiet about it. In fact, they are speaking so loudly and with such animation that people in the crowd stop to listen, amazed because each one hears someone speaking in his or her own native language.

This story reminds me of another biblical story: the tower of Babel (Genesis 11:1-9). All humanity spoke the same language at that time. They decided that they should build a tower, in hopes of physically reaching God. God confused their language so that they could no longer understand one another, thus putting an end to the building project. At Pentecost, God turned the tables. This time the various languages were for the purpose of uniting people so that they might hear the good news of Christ!

Read Acts 2:12-13.

All were amazed and perplexed, saying to one another, "What does this mean?" ¹³ But others sneered and said, "They are filled with new wine."

Some people began to question things, asking, "Aren't these folks from that little area of Galilee? How could they possibly speak any language other than their own?" Some asked, "What does this mean?" Still others, quick to judge, said, "They are drunk. The started celebrating a little early." It can be so easy for us to find other explanations rather than recognizing the work of God in our midst. We can explain almost anything away with a few well-chosen words.

Have you ever thought of Pentecost as an act of uniting? How does that idea inform your view of Pentecost?

When have you witnessed God acting but tried to come up with another explanation or cause? When have you struggled to accept God's actions?

Peter, you remember Peter? He's the one who denied even knowing Jesus. Well, he stood up and addressed the crowd, telling everyone that it was too early for them to be drunk on wine. Instead, Peter continued, the Lord had poured out his Spirit upon them as was foretold by the prophet Joel.

Read Acts 2:14-21.

But Peter, standing with the eleven, raised his voice and addressed them, "Men of Judea and all who live in Jerusalem, let this be known to you, and listen to what I say. 15 Indeed, these are not drunk, as you suppose, for it is only nine o'clock in the morning. 16 No, this is what was spoken through the prophet Joel:
17 'In the last days it will be, God declares,
that I will pour out my Spirit upon all flesh,
and your sons and your daughters shall prophesy,
and your young men shall see visions,
and your old men shall dream dreams.
18 Even upon my slaves, both men and women,
in those days I will pour out my Spirit;
and they shall prophesy.
19 And I will show portents in the heaven above
and signs on the earth below,
blood, and fire, and smoky mist.
20 The sun shall be turned to darkness
and the moon to blood,
before the coming of the Lord's great and glorious day.
21 Then everyone who calls on the name of the Lord shall be saved.'

Peter continued to address the gathered crowd, sharing the good news of Jesus. By the end of that first day, 3,000 people were not only converted, but baptized as well. After this event the disciples went out into the world, making other disciples. From this small group of followers who had gathered that day, the church was born. They spoke about their faith as the Holy Spirit led them; thousands of people heard and responded.

We often think of the miracle of Pentecost being the ways in which the Holy Spirit came to the disciples that day. But maybe the real miracle was that people heard the good news. They heard the story. Not because someone was pushing a tract into their hands or because they feared the alternative to salvation, but because the good news was presented in their own language, one they could understand. They were given the chance to hear, in a new and incredible way, that God loved them so much that he had sent his only begotten son to die for them, and they each got to hear it through the Holy Spirit's direct and personal translation.

When did you first hear the gospel in a way that you understood? To what "language" did you relate?

Workers Ahead

There are many different ways of communicating. Even though we can usually adapt to whatever form is used, we each have a preferred method of receiving and transmitting messages. For some, electronic forms of communication are the best. For others, nothing speaks to them more than a hand-written note. Some people need face-to-face contact.

My husband found his faith through Christian rock music. I found a deep connection to God through the rituals and explanations of various denominations' worship services. My parents came to a relationship with the Cumberland Presbyterian church when they were a young married couple; the church loved them and fed them as if they had always been a part of the family.

It is tempting to sit around behind closed doors, like the disciples did, and wait for something to happen. We wait for people who are like us to come through the doors. We wait for those in need to find us, even though we don't always do a good job of letting them know where help is available. Waiting is tempting, but it is not effective.

God is in the business of shaking things up, breaking down doors, stirring up wild winds. We, as the church, need to sign up to join God where these works of liberation are occurring. It is not something we can do apart from God.

From its beginning, the Cumberland Presbyterian Church has been a missional church. Our denomination got its start during a period of change. The western frontier was getting bigger by the day, and people in those western settlements were in desperate need of spiritual leadership. Meetings began popping up all over the place; tent revivals, camp meetings, and sacramental meetings peppered the landscape. At these meetings, preachers from many denominations took their place behind whatever make-shift pulpit they could find and spoke the good news that Christ had died, Christ is risen, and Christ will come again.

Thousands of people were converted and baptized during this time known as The Great Revival. During this same time, The Cumberland Presbyterian Church was born. Our founders knew first-hand the need for preachers and teachers on the frontier, and they were not afraid to bend and even break tradition to get them there. In those days, the Holy Spirit was poured out over the land in a manner very similar to what Acts chapter 2 tells us.

How does your faith community speak the "language" of people who need to know the truth about Jesus?

Does the Cumberland Presbyterian Church being rooted in a time similar to the first outpouring of the Holy Spirit change how you view your denomination? Does your faith community show ties to such a history? If so, how?

In the Rear View

There are many ways to reach out and communicate the good news, both verbal and non-verbal. There are countless programs that can be implemented, plans made, and neighborhoods canvassed with flyers. But without the Holy Spirit acting as our interpreter, all such plans are for naught.

If we are willing to let the Holy Spirit use us to fan the flame of the next great awakening, the world, our country, and your community will be forever changed. The question is, are we ready to step out into the world, anointed with fire from heaven, to speak the good news as a denomination, as a congregation, and as God's children?

Travel Log

Day 1:

"Communication is key." We hear this statement quite often. The church often struggles with how to communicate most effectively with it members and with those whom it seeks to reach. How do you personally communicate best with others? How do you best receive communication? What ways does your faith community seek to communicate its message with the community? with those outside of the community? Use whatever method you prefer to share your thoughts now.

Day 2:

There are times when words fail us. Often the best way to show our love and affection is through non-verbal means. Think of a time when someone conveyed thoughts and emotions to you without words. How did it affect you? How did you respond? Other than words, in what ways can you show others you care? Record your thoughts.

Day 3:

The Holy Spirit that came at Pentecost continues to be active in the world. When have you witnessed or felt the Holy Spirit's presence? How would you react to a dramatic entrance of the Holy Spirit into your life? Write words of thanksgiving to God for the continual presence of the Holy Spirit, or ask for assurance of the Holy Spirit's presence in your life.

Day 4:

The Holy Spirit broke into the room where the disciples were gathered, changing their lives forever. Note those areas of your life into which the Holy Spirit needs to "break" and change. How have you sought that intervention? How are you preparing for the work of the Holy Spirit to occur? Refer to your comments in a few weeks or months to see how the Holy Spirit has changed your life.

Day 5:

Peter boldly proclaimed the good news to thousands of people even though many were making negative comments about the disciples and their message. How do you react when you hear negative comments about your faith? Ask God for the words and ability to speak when it would be beneficial.

Day 6:

We often forget that the miracle of Pentecost did not occur as an isolated event, as if it had no connection to the actions of those present. The disciples had spent time with the resurrected Christ and had gathered to pray and study. Such times were essential preparation for the event of Pentecost. How are you preparing yourself to listen to and heed the Holy Spirit? What is your faith community doing to prepare to encounter both the risen Christ and the Holy Spirit? Record your responses below.

Day 7:

 The Holy Spirit acted as an interpreter on Pentecost. It allowed others to hear and understand the words of the disciples. Without the help of the Holy Spirit, God's message would not have been spread so quickly or effectively. What relationships are you struggling to understand right now? How do you need the Holy Spirit to act as interpreter for you?

www.ingramcontent.com/pod-product-compliance
Lightning Source LLC
Chambersburg PA
CBHW080937040426
42443CB00015B/3448